# Peru

## The Ultimate Peru Travel Guide By A Traveler for A Traveler

## The Best Travel Tips; Where To Go, What To See And Much More

# Table of Contents

CHAPTER 1 – A BRIEF HISTORY OF PERU

CHAPTER 2 – GEOGRAPHY AND CLIMATE OF PERU

CHAPTER 3 – THE PERUVIAN WAY OF LIFE

CHAPTER 4 – GETTING TO AND AROUND PERU

CHAPTER 5 – EXPLORE LIMA AND CENTRAL PERU

CHAPTER 6 – DISCOVER CUSCO AND THE HIGHLANDS

CHAPTER 7 – TOUR THE AMAZON

CHAPTER 8 – WHERE TO STAY

CHAPTER 9 – WHERE TO EAT

CHAPTER 10 – WHERE TO SHOP

CHAPTER 11 – WHEN TO CELEBRATE

**CONCLUSION**

# Why Lost Travelers Guides?

First, we want to wish you an amazing time in Peru when you plan to visit. Also we would like to thank you and congratulate you for downloading our travel guide, *"Peru; The Ultimate Peru Travel Guide By A Traveler For A Traveler"*.

Tired of long, boring, and biased guides out in the market that not only waste our time but also waste money? So were we! We continuously had to ask someone for the simplest things that could have easily been found if we could speak the language of the location, or information that should have been in the guide we were using at that time! As we continuously face this problem we decided we should create a guide that that would cover everything a traveler needs to know from the point of Arrival to Departure, and the Lost Travelers Guides were born.

When having our guides created we take a lot into consideration such as time, therefore our guides are short and to the point. But mainly we ask ourselves and other travelers what we enjoy during a travel and what we wish we had known prior to visiting the location and that is where the Lost Travelers guides excels. As the Lost Travelers Guide team, we only have one goal and that is to make sure that our guides are the best out, and provides the most value available.

Each one of our guides are created by a team of expert researchers and travelers whom account every detail about the location from a brief history to amazing travel tips including where to go, what to see and much more. Once our guides have been created we then go over and double check to make sure we are providing our travelers with a fun, engaging, informative and the most powerful travel guide on the market.

"The World Is A Book And Those Who Do Not Travel Only Read One Page"

- St. Augustine

Thanks again for choosing us, we hope you enjoy!

© Copyright 2016 by Seven Tree Group Inc. - All rights reserved.

This document is geared towards providing exact and reliable information in regards to the topic and issue covered. The publication is sold with the idea that the publisher is not required to render accounting, officially permitted, or otherwise, qualified services. If advice is necessary, legal or professional, a practiced individual in the profession should be ordered.

- From a Declaration of Principles which was accepted and approved equally by a Committee of the American Bar Association and a Committee of Publishers and Associations.

In no way is it legal to reproduce, duplicate, or transmit any part of this document in either electronic means or in printed format. Recording of this publication is strictly prohibited and any storage of this document is not allowed unless with written permission from the publisher. All rights reserved.

The information provided herein is stated to be truthful and consistent, in that any liability, in terms of inattention or otherwise, by any usage or abuse of any policies, processes, or directions contained within is the solitary and utter responsibility of the recipient reader. Under no circumstances will any legal responsibility or blame be held against the publisher for any reparation, damages, or monetary loss due to the information herein, either directly or indirectly.

Respective authors own all copyrights not held by the publisher.

The information herein is offered for informational purposes solely, and is universal as so. The presentation of the information is without contract or any type of guarantee assurance.

The trademarks that are used are without any consent, and the publication of the trademark is without permission or backing by the trademark owner. All trademarks and brands within this book are for clarifying purposes only and are the owned by the owners themselves, not affiliated with this document.

# Chapter 1 – A Brief History of Peru

Peru with its vastness of archeological wealth is incomparable. For some reason when people hear about Peruvian history, they immediately think about the story of Inca civilization. It is probably what Peru is most known for. But the truth is Peruvian history has intricate weavings. Its history is much more complex, it goes deeper than the Inca. It goes as far back as millennia. So, let's explore Peruvian history starting from the pre-ceramic period.

**The Early Inhabitants**

Around 20,000 years ago when humans migrated across the Bering Strait, some nomadic hunters and gatherers landed in Peru. They came to the country roaming in loose-knit bands. The early inhabitants lived in caves. They hunted mastodons, saber-toothed tigers, giant sloths and other fearsome animals. The existence and lifestyle of the early inhabitants were found in cave paintings that depict hunting scenes discovered in Toquepala and Lauricocha.

In 4000 BC, the inhabitants began to domesticate guinea pigs, alpaca and llama. Others suggest that it may have started way back in 7000 BC. Around this time too, people have begun planting seeds. They no longer relied solely on hunting for food. The people learned simple horticultural methods to improve their crops.

Today, Peru's coastal strip is a desert. Back then however, it was wetter. As a matter of fact, there were small settlements here. People tilled the land and planted crops like corn, squash, cotton, quinoa, beans and potato. They also fished using bone hooks and nets. They lived on sea lions, seabird eggs, sea urchins and shellfish. The people twined cotton to make their clothing; later though, they learned to apply weaving techniques.

Trade occurred in the Amazon basin. Evidences of trade relations between the Amazon and Andean regions include cassava, sweet potatoes, rainforest bird feathers and coca leaf among others. Although metalwork and ceramics were yet to be discovered by people in this period, they did craft jewelry from shell and bone.

The inhabitants of the coastal area built simple dwellings from reeds and branches with stone lining. They also built structures meant for rituals and ceremonies. The most complex and unique perhaps were the Caral ruins built around 3000 BC. There were astronomical observatories as well. The ruins of the oldest one were discovered north of Lima.

People also settled in the highlands. Although little is known about how these people lived, the structures they built are considered to be the most developed from this period. The earliest ruins from the highland settlers were found near Huánuco.

Organized life in Peru did not occur until the 2500 BC. Early Peruvian civilization evolved in the next 1500 years. During these times, various organized cultures emerged like the Chavìn and the Sechìn. The Chavìn were responsible for stylized religious iconography. Their influence spread to the whole coastal region. The Sechìn on the other hand, may not have had many cultural achievements but they are equally memorable for their military hegemony.

The Chavìn and the Sechìn culture and influence eventually declined which paved the way for the development of other regional cultures like the Saliner and the Paracas. These cultures were responsible for technological and artistic advances. They came up with weaving techniques which were more sophisticated than that of their predecessors. They also learned to make kiln-fired ceramics. After the Paracas, the Nazca emerged. We know the Nazca today for leaving a visible legacy. That is the cryptic and immense Nazca Lines.

## The Inca Empire

The early inhabitants of Peru may be responsible for many cultural, artistic, military and technological advances. However, their accomplishments would seem inferior when compared to that of the Inca.

Around 1430, the Inca's realm only consisted of the river valley surrounding Cuzco. Because of their brevity however, they managed to expand their realm immensely to nearly 1 million square kilometers in less than a century. This means their influence and rule extended beyond Peru. They reigned from the northwest of Argentina up to the southern part of Colombia. To ensure their reign over the conquered territories, the Incas impose their way of life on their subjects.

The capital of the Inca Empire was Qosqo. It was the wealthiest city on the Americas with all their glorious temples adorned in heavy gold plate. Although only fragments of their architectural magnificence are left now, they are still astounding. You will find some of these magnificent fragments in Macchu Picchu.

## Then the Spaniards Came

Because of an epidemic, the 11th Inca (king), Huayna Capac split the territory between his sons born of different mothers, Atahualpa and Huascar, believing that it was the best way to avoid conflict. Atahualpa took the north and Huascar took the south. Unfortunately the 11th Inca was wrong. War between the brothers started. It took years before one emerged as the victor. By that time, the Spanish were ready to take over.

While the north and the south were busy fighting in their civil war, Francisco Pizarro had discovered the wealth of the Inca Empire in 1528. He was astonished at the sight of the Inca's coastal settlements. He decided to go home and gather enough forces for a conquest. True enough, Pizarro returned and buried a Spanish flag in a town in Peru in September 1532. He named it San Miguel de Piura.

The Inca Empire was at the height of its power in 1532. Atahualpa just defeated his half brother so the empire is once again united under a single rule. Unfortunately, the new Inca was outsmarted leading to his demise and that of the entire empire. Pizarro requested an audience with Atahualpa which was granted. What was supposed to be a meeting turned out to be an ambush.

Atahualpa was captured and thousands of tribes people, unarmed, were killed. Pizarro and his troops made ransom requests. Because of the desire to gain their freedom and their leader back, the Incas offered ransom in the form of gold and silver. Some of which were literally stripped off from what used to be the most glorious temple the Inca empire had ever built, the Qorikancha. It turned out to be another trick from Pizarro. He killed the Atahualpa and marched forward bringing the great empire down to its knees.

**The Spanish Rule**

The Incas made several attempts to recover their territories. None of those attempts were successful however. Peru was in great turmoil for the next 30 years with the Spaniards fighting among themselves for control. After the last Inca was defeated and Pizarro was assassinated, the next 200 years became more peaceful.

Lima was declared as the capital. The Spaniards called it "City of Kings." They groomed Lima to become the commercial, social and political center of the Andean nations. The Spanish also built colonial churches in the highlands and a school of art in Cuzco.

The 19th century marked the beginning of revolutions as the people of South America grew more dissatisfied with the Spanish rule. Peru along with other South American colonies was freed. The Spanish fought in defense but finally surrendered in 1826.

After the war with Spain, things were still shaky for Peru as they also fought a war against Ecuador over border dispute.

The 20th century was a period of military dictatorship and revolutions. The political instability in Peru ended in the 90s. This sustained period of peace opened Peru up for tourism. Adventure seekers from all over the world come to Peru to admire its complex heritage and undeniable beauty.

# Chapter 2 – Geography and Climate of Peru

Found in the west of South America, Peru covers a vast area of 1,285,215 square kilometers of land with 60 million hectares of the Antarctic and 200 nautical miles of the Pacific. This means Peru the third largest country in the continent. It has a population of 23 million.

Peru is a country of diversity not only because of its multi-layered culture and history but also because of its geography. It consists of 11 different ecological regions. Out of the 117 varying life zones in the world, 84 can be found in this country. This geographical diversity blessed the country with a variety of beautiful scenery. It also provides Peru with a deep source of natural resources. Based on the traditional method, Peru can be divided into three main regions: the mountains, the coast and the jungle.

**The Highlands**

The highlands make up 30 percent of Peru with 36 percent of the population residing here. The Andes mountain range dominates this mountainous region. It is blessed with various altitudes and different ecological regions. Because of its lower location, the northern area of the Andes is a little more humid than the rest of the highlands. The central Andes are the steepest and tallest. This is where you'll find the Huascarán which is also known as the highest peak measuring at 6,768 meters above sea level. While the central area is the tallest, the southern area has a wider land area. It is also referred to as the high Andean plateau or altiplano.

The highlands of Peru have two seasons, winter and summer. Winter is between November and March. It is characterized by heavy rains. With daylight, temperature is around 24°C but at night, it can fall as low as -3°C.

Summer begins in April and ends in October. There is little rain during this time. The days are sunny and the nights are cold. If you want to pay the historic highlands of Peru a visit, this is the best time to do so.

The inhabitants of the highlands rely heavily on agriculture for subsistence. It is also not as progressive as the cosmopolitan area. In fact, it is marked by poverty. The people here live a simple life away from the comforts of the modern city. But this characteristic is also what makes it attractive for tourists who seek adventure and relief from modernity.

## The Coast

Consisting 11 percent of Peru's national territory, the coast is made up of fertile valleys, narrow deserts and wide beaches. 50 percent of the population resides here. The fertile lowlands have become the center of the country. It has a wealthy cosmopolitan culture.

The region has a forgiving climate. Its weather is warm-temperate. The southern area can be very humid in summer reaching up to 30°C. Then, it becomes foggy and cold in winter. The northern area of the coast on the other hand, is hot and sunny throughout the year although it rains in November and December.

## The Jungle

The Amazon rainforest is found in the east of Peru. It makes up 59 percent of Peru's national territory consisting of tropical vegetation and natural reserves. It is home to around 12 percent of the population.

The summer is undoubtedly the best time to explore this region. From April to October, the roads are much more accessible and the rivers subside. The weather is fairly humid throughout the year except in between May and August when the wind carries cold snaps from the south. They call this *surazos* or *friajes*. During these cold snaps, the temperature can fall to 12°C, sometimes reaching as low as 8°C. The winter season begins in November and ends in March.

## Best time to visit Peru?

You've learned that the weather varies in Peru according to the region. The weather is nicest from April to October in all of the Peruvian regions so it is the best time to explore the beautiful country. However, this is also when thousands of other tourists fly in. The high peak tourist season means more expensive plane tickets and hotel accommodation. But it also means nicer weather and safer for exploring the highlands and the jungle.

If you are planning on staying in the coastal region however, and want to avoid the tourist traffic, you can go anytime of the year. The weather may be slightly damp, cold and overcast from June to September but it barely rains in this part of Peru.

## What to pack?

If you're travelling to and around Peru, you need to pack a variety of clothes. If you're going in the summer, you need lightweight clothes for the coast and thicker ones because it can get very cold in the highlands especially when the sun falls. While you'd be more comfortable wearing sandals or flip flops in the beach, you will need supportive boots if you plan to explore the jungle or go mountain hiking.

If you're travelling between March and September, you should come prepared for the cold surges and pack a jumper. Expect the sky to cry during the rainy season so bring waterproof clothing. For the winter, you will need ski jackets, hats, gloves and thermals to survive the freezing nights in the highlands.

# Chapter 3 – The Peruvian Way of Life

Peruvian culture is heavily influenced by the early settlers, the native Incas and the Spanish conquistadores. They have inherited their ancestors' customs, beliefs and way of life. Europeans, Japanese, Africans, Chinese and other immigrant groups also have contributed to this culture. Although Peruvians have different ethnic backgrounds, they are united and in complete agreement when it comes to the importance of religion and family. As a matter of fact, generations of a family typically live under one roof. The younger generation care for their elderly. Being closely-knit, Peruvian families help each other out especially in challenging times.

The Peruvians keep their traditions and customs alive through various art forms, music, dance, food, sports, religion, education, clothing, etc.

**Peruvian Arts and Crafts**

Since the pre-Inca times, the people of Peru had been skilled craftsmen. The tradition still thrives today. There are native Amerindians in Peru who still spin sheep wool, alpaca, llama and cotton into yarn. Just like their ancestors, they weave the yarn to make clothing or a textile. These people do not just weave wool. They also weave reeds, particularly the inhabitants of the floating islands of Titicaca Lake. They use the reeds they weaved to build their houses and the islands where they reside. Every village of this area uses distinctive patterns and colors.

The Peruvians are also known for making gold and silver jewelry as well as wood carvings. Craftsmen from Ayacucho make colorful wooden altars called retablos. They carve figurines of everyday scenes and religious depiction into the wood. The retablos come from Spanish conquistadores influence. Peruvian pottery on the other hand, reflects the traditions of the ancient Moche and Nazca. You will find many of these arts and crafts from markets. Tourists buy them as souvenirs.

The paintings and sculptures from the colonial period adorn the churches of Peru. In the 17th and 18th centuries, there are native Peruvian painters who also emerged in the art scene. They called themselves the Cuzco school of painters. The most popular of them all was Diego Quispe Tito. The art works of this era were focused on either a religion theme or local landscape. 19th century painters focused on battles, war and heroes, inspired by the challenges the country and the people went through during this period. Modern Peruvian art is mostly abstract. The most renowned modern painter and sculptor are Fernando de Szyslo and Joaquin Roca Rey respectively.

**Music and Dance**

There is no Peruvian party unless there is music and dance. The music from the coast and the Andean music are quite different. The Andeans use panpipes and flutes to make sweet sounds. They also use violins, harps and charango to accompany native drums, wind and brass instruments. As for dance, the Andeans have over 300 different dances but the most notorious one is called huayno. With colorful costumes on, the dancers stamp their feet vigorously to the music.

The coastal people, on the other hand, are renowned for their Criollo music originating from African and Spanish rhythms. This music is used to accompany the Peruvian marinera which is a traditional courtship dance performed with the use of handkerchiefs. Another popular type of music from the coast is the chicha. It is a combination of Andean and Afro-Peruvian beats.

**Food**

Each region has its specialty. Because the coastal region is rich in seafood, their cuisine is focused on this resource. The Andean cuisine on the other hand, uses mainly meat and potatoes while those in the Amazon are famous for their tropical fruits and river fish dishes.

## Sports

This is a nation crazy for soccer. It is the Peruvians national sport. Every school age child plays it. They call it "futbol". Residents from the coast however, are more into of surfing because of their access to massive waves. The Chicama Beach is known in the world over for having the longest waves.

Bullfighting is still embedded in Peruvian tradition, a tradition they inherited from the Spaniards. Bullfighting is held at Plaza de Acho which is known as the the oldest bullring in all of the Americas.

## Religion

If you find a plaza in the city, there is more likely a church near it. 90 percent of Peruvians is Roman Catholic. This does not mean the Peruvians completely disregard the religion and spiritual beliefs of their ancestors. There are still tribes in the Amazon however, that practice ancient religion. Although most of the Peruvian festivals revolve around Christianity, there are some that are still upheld in honor of the Inca and other early religions.

# Chapter 4 – Getting To and Around Peru

Getting to Peru is easier than getting around it. There are four ways to reach Peru, by air, by land, by rail and by water.

## By Plane

Overseas flights land at Lima's Jorge Chávez International Airport. If you're flying to, from or around the country, you should know that reconfirmation of flights is a requirement.

International flights must be reconfirmed by passengers 72 hours before the travel time while domestic flights must be reconfirmed 48 hours ahead of travel. Passengers must arrive at the airport at least 2 hours before the scheduled flight. Taxes are also applicable. Airport tax on international flights is at $31 and $6 for local flights. The tax must be settled before boarding. It must be paid in cash either in US dollar or Peruvian Nuevos Soles.

## By Bus

If you're coming from Chile, Bolivia or Ecuador, you can also get to Peru by bus. Traveling by land is time consuming but it can be much cheaper. The bus from Guayaquil or Quito to Lima will pass by the major coastal cities. On the other hand, buses from Bolivia arrive at Puno then to Cusco. Most buses from Chile arrive at Tacna and from there you can hop on to another bus to get to Lima or Arequipa.

## By Rail

You can also access Peru through the international rail service. There is only one route. It will take you from Arica, border of northern Chile to Tacna in the south of Peru. The journey is about 90 minutes long. Note that there are only a few rail routes in the country. It will be wise to book your train tickets in advance, at least a day before traveling.

## By Boat

The main ports in Peru are San Martín and Callao. There are a few international cruises as well. If you want to reach Peru through Brazil, you can get through to the Amazon basin and arrive at the main river port which is at Iquitos.

Cruise ships usually stop at Callao in Lima, Salaverry in Trujillo or Matarani which is near Arequipa. The stop is rather brief. The main disadvantage is that these cruises will not give you access to the major attractions of Peru which are located in high altitudes.

Getting to Peru is half the battle. Why is it more challenging to get around Peru than to get there? The answer is quite simple. This country is vast and made more complex by natural barriers such as desert coast, rainforest, mountain terrains, etc. Needless to say, Peru is not easy to navigate especially for a first time traveler. It does not mean navigating through the country is impossible though. Here are some of the ways you can get around this beautiful country.

## By Plane

Flying is absolutely recommended if you only have a few weeks or less to explore Peru. Major cities can be reached by plane. Some major destinations may require additional overland trip but it is still less time consuming to fly. Also, there are major attractions that can only be reached by plane like some areas in the jungle including Iquitos.

A one-way flight to major destinations like Iquitos, Puerto Maldonado, Arequipa, Cusco and Lima can cost anywhere between $89 and $219. The airfare may vary according to the season. To get to Puno, you have to fly to arrive at Juliaca and from Juliaca, continue the journey by land.

For more information on airfare, flight schedules and routes, you can look up or contact the following small airlines.

LAN (www.lan.com; T: 866/435-9526 or 01/213-8200 in Lima or 305/670-9999 in the US)

Peruvian Airlines (www.peruvianairlines.pe; T: 01/716-6000)

TACA Airlines (www.taca.com; T: 01/511-8222 in Lima or 800/400-TACA [8222] in the US)

Star Perú (www.starperu.com; T: 01/705-9000)

LC Busre (www.lcbusre.com.pe; T: 01/619-1313)

**By Train**

If you have more time to spare then you should take the train and be treated on a scenic journey. Be warned however, that luggage theft is still an issue on Peruvian trains. In which case, you may want to travel lightly or opt for the premium-class ticket. The PeruRail from Cusco to Machu Picchu is one of the exciting journeys with the most spectacular views.

The Andean Railways and Inca Rail companies also have trips from the Sacred Valley heading to Machu Picchu. Another popular trip is the PeruRail Titicaca Route from Cusco to Puno. It stops at Juliaca en route. However, it is not for people in a hurry to get to the destination. The journey is pricey and slow. That's because it is meant to take tourist through the scenic views.

Train passes are not available but you can get more information through the following.

*PeruRail (T: 084/581-414 in Cusco or 01/612-6700 in Lima)*

*Machu Picchu Train (www.machupicchutrain.com; T: 084/221-199)*

*Inca Rail (www.incarail.com; T: 084/233-030)*

For a high altitude journey, you can take the Ferrocarril Central Andino S.A. from Lima to Huancayo. It does not operate daily however. If you want to be on board on this journey, make sure to inquire by phone at telephone number, 01/226-6363 or check out their website at www.ferrocarrilcentral.com.pe for updates.

## By Taxi

One of the most convenient ways to get around the cities of Peru is through taxi. However, it is also one of the most expensive modes of transportation. There are unregulated taxis. These are private cars that have small taxi stickers stuck in the windshield. For a safer travel, you should look for the regulated taxis. These are the ones with a company number lit on the roof. Taxis called for service by phone is generally more expensive but are far more reliable than those flagged down on the street.

Taxis in Peru do not have meters in them. In which case, you have to negotiate with the driver on the fare before getting in, especially if you are taking a long trip. For short trips, the standard fare in most cities is $5. Tipping is not a requirement unless you are feeling generous or completely satisfied with the service.

## By Bus

Buses are the most preferred means of transportation in Peru. They are crowded and slow but the fares are quite cheap. There are a few luxury buses for long-distance trips. The fare costs twice as much as regular buses but they are safer and more comfortable. Because of the long list of bus operators, destinations and terminals, it is best to consult with local tourism information office or travel agency for more information. Among the most trusted bus companies for long-distance journeys include the following.

*Civa (www.civa.com.pe; T: 01/418-1111)*

*Oltursa (www.oltursa.com.pe; T: 01/708-5000)*

*Cruz del Sur (www.cruzdelsur.com.pe; T: 01/311-5050)*

*Ormeño (www.grupo-ormeno.com.pe; T: 01/472-5000)*

## By Car

You can also rent a car to get around Peru but given the aggressive nature of drivers and the condition of the roads, it may not be the best option, especially around Lima. If you are traveling outside Cusco however, and sharing the cost with other tourists, car rental is a decent option. Car rental costs for economy-sized vehicles range between $40 and $70 a day with additional 18 percent for insurance. The major car rental companies in Peru include the following.

*Paz Rent a Car (T: 01/436-3941)*

*InterService Rent a Car (T: 01/442-2256)*

*National Car Rental (www.nationalcar.com; T: 01/433-3750)*

*Hertz (www.hertz.com; T: 01/575-1390)*

*Dollar (www.dollar.com; T: 01/444-3050)*

*Budget (www.budget.com; T: 01/575-1674)*

*Avis (www.avis.com; T: 01/575-0912 ext. 4155)*

If you need mechanical assistance, you can contact the Touring Club of Peru (Touring Automóvil Club del Perú) in Lima at phone number, 01/221-3225 or in Cusco at phone number, 084/224-561.

## By Private Bus

If you prefer a faster means of transportation than buses and cheaper than taxis, private bus services or combis are also available. Some travel between cities and others cover longer distances. Fare is paid through a money collector or cobrador on board. Because combis are usually crowded, pickpocketing is a problem so take care of your valuables. You don't have to go to the station to get on one. You can just flag one down from the streets.

## By Bike

Cycling around Peru is only advisable in the coastal paths. Cycling in the mountains is dangerous. The roads and the distances are not forgiving. Rent a bike only if you want a cheaper means to get around Cusco, Huaraz or Lima.

## By Boat

You can travel between Pucallpa and Iquitos or Yurimaguas and Iquitos by boat. Depending on the destination, travel time can take 2 to 7 days. Water transportation is not only more time consuming. They are also sporadic and generally uncomfortable.

## On Foot

If everything else fails, you can also get around Peru on foot. Expect to do some walking even if you have no intention to hike because most of the beautiful attraction can only be accessed on foot. Wear running shoes or better yet hiking boots that provide good ankle support.

If you have heavy luggage, you can hire llamas which can carry 25 to 30 kg of weight. They move rather slowly though. A burro or donkey can carry a heavier load up to 80kg but the most commonly hired animal are mules. Hiring mules starts at $5 for the entire day. The animal comes with an arriero who can also serve as your guide. Horses and mules are also available for riding but hiring one usually cost much more.

# Chapter 5 – Explore Lima and Central Peru

Peru is a pretty huge country. For the purpose of simplicity, we will cover the best sights and best experiences according to region and city or town starting with Central Peru which includes the capital Lima, Pasco, Callao, Ucayali, Huancavelica, Huanuco, Junin and Ancash.

## Lima

A world heritage site, Lima is the oldest civilization in America. The Spanish conquistadores left a visible mark in the city but Lima's history actually dates back to the pre-colonial era. Modernity did not diminish Lima's historical value. The colonial mansions with their epic balconies, centuries old monasteries and churches are well preserved. There are various things to experience in this city from beaches to valleys, art museums to boardwalks, adventure sports to nightlife, archeological sites to natural reserves.

*Weather in Lima*: The climate is usually warm and dry especially in areas near the coast. Minimum temperature is at 14°C (or 57°F) and maximum temperature is at 27°C (or 81°F).

### *What to see in Lima*

**Lima Plaza Mayor** - If you're in Lima, do not forget to explore the historic center which includes the Lima Plaza Mayor. The highlight of the main square is the 17th century bronze fountain. You can stop by anytime of the day and night to soak in the beauty of this historical site.

**Lima Cathedral** - Found in the Plaza Mayor, the Lima Cathedral is a sight to behold. Its interior may be austere but it houses historic jewels which includes Francisco Pizarro's remains, Baltasar Noguera side altars and choir stalls. The Cathedral is open from Mondays to Saturdays between 9am and 5pm as well as on Saturdays from 10am to 1pm. While you're in the area, you may also want to check out the Museum of Religious Art for the vast collection of chasubles, chalices, sculptures and paintings.

***Government Palace*** - Also located along Lima Plaza Mayor, the Government Palace used to be Francisco Pizarro's residence. In its halls and yards are adorned with valuable figures of Peruvian history along with magnificent art works. To visit and explore this wondrous palace, prior arrangement must be made.

***San Francisco Church and Convent*** - Located in Jr. Ancash Block 3, this site holds a group of 17th century structures including a plaza, church and convent. The main façade featuring Corinthian columns is built from stone. Its open cornice and beautiful arch contains a depiction of the Immaculate Conception. While you're here, you can also drop by at the Museum of Vice-Royalty Art and catacombs or subterranean galleries which served as a cemetery in the colonial times.

***Gastronomy House*** - Are you curious about the history of Peruvian cuisine? This museum located at Jirón Conde de Superunda No 170 can take you through the 500-year of history of this culture's cuisine. It is right next to the Government Palace. The museum is open from Tuesday to Sunday between 9am and 5pm. The best part is, admission is absolutely free.

***Caral Sacred City*** - Located at km 184 on the Panamericana Norte around 206km north of Lima, the Caral Sacred City is a UNESCO World Heritage Site. It is the most ancient civilization in the country and in the Americas. It is approximately 5,000 years old. Early inhabitants used this place for worship and trade. Visit the Sacred City during daytime to fully enjoy the view.

***Pachacámac Archaeological Complex*** - Located in Lurín, this was the commercial center during the pre-Inca times. You will find several structures built in mud like temples, plazas and palaces. The highlights of this archeological complex however, are the Acllahuasi and the Temple of the Sun. You can also visit the on-site museum which houses the excavated items from the Inca era. The museum is open daily from 9am to 4pm.

## What to Eat in Lima

Lima has plenty of specialty dishes. Among the must-try include the following.

***Tacu-tacu*** - This refried bean dish is served with breaded beef and rice with a drizzle of onion sauce.

***Lomo saltado*** - Stir fried beef with onions, chilies, tomatoes and herbs can be enjoyed with rice and fries.

***Carapulcra*** - Steamed potatoes stewed with chicken and pork may sound ordinary. The superb combination of chilies and spices make it extra special.

***Choritos a la chalaca*** - Mussels dish drizzled with lemon juice and seasoned with chili pepper and onions.

***Anticuchos*** - This is roasted cow heart marinated in vinegar and Panca chilies.

***Escabeche*** - This is pickled protein. Chicken or fish is marinated in vinegar first then slow cooked in onions.

***Causa rellena*** - This is potato pasta with ground chili seasoning and chicken or tuna filling.

# Pasco

A place of contrast, Pasco is where the mountains and the jungle meet. If you are looking for an adventure, this is the place to be. With its diverse flora and fauna along with its magnificent waterfalls, it is also a perfect spot for nature lovers.

*Weather in Pasco* - It is slightly humid, cold and wet. The maximum temperature is at 12°C (or 54°F) and minimum temperature of -2°C (or 28°F).

## What to See in Pasco

**La Calera Hot Springs** - The thermal baths are like no other reaching up to 60 °C of temperature. Located 43 km northwest of the city of Cerro de Pasco, La Calera Hot Springs are rich in bicarbonates, sulphates, chlorides, magnesium, potassium and calcium. The therapeutic waters are ideal for treating nervous conditions and muscular pain. You can soak in the warm bath during daytime.

**Punrun Lagoon** - Located 37 km south-west of Pasco, this beautiful lagoon measures 8 sq km with a depth of 200 meters. The cold water has five islands but the jewel lies in the Pumapachupan. The shores have diverse flora. It is also home to various bird species, trout, frogs, catfish and carachi fich.

**Huayllay National Sanctuary** - 45 km south of Pasco, Huayllay National Sanctuary features rock formations of different sizes and shapes. You will find hot springs in the forest as well with various therapeutic properties. Flora life consists of mata mata trees, putaga, queñua and huamanpinta among others. The area is home to quails, sparrow hawks, wildcats, vizcachas and vicuñas among many others. The sanctuary is open to visitors daily from 8am to 5:30pm. The area is also open for camping.

## What to Eat in Pasco

***Picante de cuy*** - It literally means spicy guinea pig. The meat is fried and served with sauce made from green onions, red chili peppers and peanuts.

***Pachamanca*** - Made from different types of meat, this dish also uses cooked corn, sweet corn and potatoes seasoned with various aromatic herbs. Pachamanca is prepared using a pre-Hispanic style of cooking. That is in a hole covered with soil and sandwiched between hot rocks.

***Jora chicha*** - Peruvians have been drinking this beverage made from macerated corn since the pre-Inca times.


## Other Notable Attractions in Central Peru

*Uchkus Inkañan Archaeological Complex* - Found in Huancavelica, this archeological complex served as a religious, administrative and astronomical observation center. For instance, one platform has water mirrors used to monitor the movement of the sun and the moon. There are miniature terraces found here as well which are believed to have served as an experimentation field for growing different crops back in the ancient times.

**Chonta Peak** - Also in Huancavelica, Chonta peak is less than 2 hours away from the city center by car. You can enjoy this spot not only for its striking landscapes. It is also one of the best spots in Peru for adventure sports.

***Izcuchaca District*** - Tourists visit this place not only for its overwhelming number of therapeutic hot springs located in Aguas Calientes, Huaspu and Paucari. The Izcuchaca district is also known for its traditional potters and handicraft makers. Stop by for remarkable souvenirs then proceed to the highest areas of the district where you can marvel at Pre-Inca and Inca ruins.

***The Pultocc Lagoon*** - Home of the Andean flamingos, wild ducks, trout and other livestock, this lagoon is not only famous for its wildlife abundance. Its views are also just as fascinating surrounded by mountains covered in snow, a striking contrast against the deep blue water.

# Chapter 6 – Discover Cusco and the Highlands

Also known as the navel of the world, Cusco is natural, striking and seductive. If you want to experience the living culture of Peru, go on an exciting adventure and be close to nature, Cusco is a must see. It boasts of various archeological sites, religious monuments, architectural prowess from Inca stonemasons, intricate handicraft collections, popular traditions and diverse flora and fauna.

*Weather in Cusco*: The city has a cold and semi-dry climate. Minimum temperature can reach as low as 1°C (or 34°F) and maximum temperature at 21°C (or 70°F).

## What to See in Cusco

**Cuzco Plaza de Armas** – Before the Spaniards came, this was a ceremonial site. The Incas celebrated the Inti Raymi or the Festival of the Sun here. When Francisco Pizarro came and conquered the city, this is where he proclaimed victory. In the colonial era, the Spaniards built structures and stone arches in the plaza. These colonial structures remain standing today. You can visit Cuzco Plaza de Armas either at day or night.

**Cuzco Cathedral** - Found in Plaza de Armas, the Cuzco Cathedral is built according to Renaissance style. The interior features exquisite carvings in alder and cedar. Visitors will also find important painting collections here from the Cuzco school as well as silver-embossed objects. In addition to these collections, you will also find remarkably beautiful pulpit and choir here. The cathedral is open from Tuesdays to Sundays between 10am and 6pm.

**Temple of La Compañía de Jesús** - Also located in Plaza de Armas, this temple was originally built in 1571. It was rebuilt in 1688 after it was destroyed by the 1650 earthquake. Temple of La Compañía de Jesús is a perfect example of Andean Baroque style.

The altar pieces are skillfully sculpted notable of Baroque, churrigueresco and plateresque styles. The highlights of the temple include the three part columns, the wooden pulpit and "The Marriage of Martín García de Loyola to Beatriz Clara Coya." Visiting hours is between Monday and Friday from 9am to 5pm. It is also open on Saturdays and Sundays from 9am to 11am and 1pm to 5pm.

**San Blas neighborhood** - Only four blocks away from Plaza de Armas, this area is also known as the Artisan's neighborhood. The narrow and steep streets along with the houses are reminiscent of the colonial era. It is best to explore this neighborhood during daytime.

Outside the city center of Cusco, you will find planty of archeological complexes. Here are a couple of them.

**Sacsayhuamán Archaeological Complex** - This site is only 2 km away from north-east of Cusco. It holds a sum of 33 archeological sites. The most popular is the Sacsayhuaman Fortress, which served as a religious site. According to historians, the fortress was probably built by the end of 14th century or at the beginning of the 15th century under Inca Pachactueq.

Experts consider it a cyclopean construction because of the enormous sizes of the stones used for building the structure. Today, this is where the Peruvians celebrate Inti Raymi every 24th of June. You can visit the complex daily from 7am to 6pm.

**Qenko archaeological complex** - The name Qenko means "labyrinth." It used to be a sacred place where the early inhabitants gather for religious ceremonies. It was built in honor of the Sun, moon and stars. It is open daily from 7am to 6pm, only 10 minutes away from the city center.

**Puka Pukara Archaeological Complex** - Historians believe this site used to be lodging for the Inca's large committee. Legend has it that every time the Inca went to visit

Tambomachay, his entourage would stay in this lodging area. You can reach the Puka Pukara in 15 minutes from the city center by car or 2 hours on foot.

***Tambomachay Archaeological* Complex** - Only 20 minutes away from the city center of Cusco, Tambomachay played a crucial religious role associated to water and regeneration. The complex is more than half a hectare wide. The Incas constructed Tambomachay using polygon-shaped limestone. The site is open daily from 7am to 6pm.

***Inca Trail to Machu Picchu*** - For most tourists, this is the top reason for visiting the country. If you want to take this trail, you should schedule your Peru vacation between March and January. There are various circuits to explore based on the actual session you would like to focus on. Among the most popular but strenuous routes begins at km 82 following the Cusco-Machu Picchu rail line. There is an alternative and less strenuous route, the Camino Sagrado or Sacred Path. The route begins at km 104 following the same rail line.

On your way up to Machu Picchu, you can enjoy the view of flowing water from glaciers and plenty of ravines. There are numerous archeological sites here. Among the most important ones are Wiñayhuayna, Qoriwachayrachina, Runkuraqay, Patallaqta, Sayacmarca, Intipata, Phuyupatamarca and Intipunku.

## *What to Eat in Cusco*

***Humita*** - Prepared using fresh corn filling with corn leaves wrap, humita is either baked or steamed and can be made savory or sweet.

***Adobo*** - Before being cooked in a pot, the pork is marinated first in spices and fermented corn which the locals call chicha.

***Tamal*** - Like the humita, tamal is a sweet or savory dish made from corn filling with corn leaves as wrapping. The difference is tamal is made from dry corn, not fresh corn as used in Humita.

***Kapchi*** - It is basically a broth made from cheese, eggs, milk and broad beans. Sometimes, mushrooms and potatoes are also used as ingredients.

## Other Notable Attractions in Southern Peru

***The Colca Valley in Arequipa*** - A valley with many names, Colca Valley is also called as 'The Valley of Fire', 'The Lost Valley of the Incas', 'The Valley of Wonders' and a bunch of other aliases. Residents of Colca are notable with their colorful and intricately designed clothing as well as their ribbon decorated hats. The best attraction of the valley by far is the magnificent Colca Canyon which is two times deeper than the Grand Canyon. This is home to the striking Andean Condors with their 10 foot wing span.

***The Nazca Lines*** - If there is one word that can describe these lines, it's "mystifying." Geoglyphs that depict spider, condor and monkey among others are etched into the desert floor. The Nazca lines is believed to have been made anywhere between 500 BC and 500 AD. It is still a mystery why and who made the lines but it is certainly a striking vision.

***Lake Titicaca*** - The largest lake in South America, Lake Titicaca is believed to be the birthplace of the sun. This is why the lake itself and its islands are regarded as sacred. Being isolated from the big cities, traditional culture is much alive here. As a matter of fact, villagers still speak Quecha, the ancient Inca language.

Among the most popular islands in Lake Titicaca are Amantani and Taquile. The man-made Uros Islands made from floating totora seeds are also not to be missed.

# Chapter 7 – Tour the Amazon

Northern Peru is often overlooked. Many tourists prefer the more accessible South and Central regions of the country. This does not take away from the beauty and magnificence of this far-flung region. Those who allot some time and dedicate their energy to travel through the Amazon and the rest of Northern Peru are lucky to do so. The journey is not glamorous but the experience is unforgettable for all the glory of the North.

## Iquitos

Known as the gateway to the Amazon basin, Iquitos is also full of surprises. You can take the time here to explore the villages where tribes people live, immerse yourself in their way of life and be charmed by their culture, food, exotic goods and floating huts.

### *What to See in Iquitos*

**Belén** - You will find this floating village at the southeast end of Iquitos. Huts are built on rafts and they move to the rhythm of the river. To date, there are around seven thousand villagers. These villagers use canoes to move from hut to hut to trade. The best time to pay Belén a visit is at 7 in the morning so you can witness the villagers take their produce around.

While you're in Belén, you might as well visit the Belén mercado where anything from the most mundane products to the strangest, most exotic ones are sold. You may want to take home chuchuhuasi or other Amazon plants which are used as tonics for the most common ailments.

**Yaguas and Boras** - These are two real Indian tribes. The natives still live the way their ancestors lived hundreds of years ago. If you're lucky, you may just see the Boras perform their traditional dances. If you're luckier, you may get a lesson on how to shoot with the blow gun from the Yaguas. You can also buy handicraft goods from both tribes here made of jungle-extracted products.

***Pilpintuwasi Butterfly Farm*** - Home to Amazonian butterflies like the blue morpho and the owl butterfly, Pilpintuwasi is not all about the striking butterflies though. Among the residents of the farm include anteater, tapir and mischievous monkeys freely roaming around. You will also see majestic jaguars here. Admission to the farm costs $20. You can get more information at, www.amazonanimalorphanage.org

***Quistococha Zoological Park*** - Are curious about rainforest wildlife? You can learn a lot from Quistococha Zoological Park. The park houses wild animals like a marguay, ocelot or jaguar that you are less likely to see in the wild because of their nocturnal nature. The park also has an aviary, botanical garden and serpentarium. To cool off, guests are allowed to swim in the lake with beach.

***Pink Dolphin*** - Found in the Amazon, this is probably the most popular wildlife in the region. This special kind of dolphins is frequently spotted in this area. Watch out for one as you take a Boat ride through the rivers of Iquitos.

## What to Eat

***Milk liqueur*** - This is a combination of milk whey and sugar cane spirit. The ingredients are filtered to the last drop so they become transparent.

***Humitas*** - This is corn filling mixed with either cheese or seasoned meat, wrapped with corn leaves before it is steam-cooked.

## Other Notable Attractions in Northern Peru

***Chan Chan*** - One of the most famous ancient treasures in Peru, Chan Chan used to be the capital of the Chimú kingdom that ruled before the Incas. Amount the highlights of this archeological complex include the citadels with its intricate details and decorative walls adorned with various motifs from fish and birds to geometrical patterns. This tourist spot is 10 minutes away from the city of Trujillo in Northern Peru.

***Kuélap Archaeological Complex*** - An imposing fortress constructed by the pre-Inca culture of the Chachapoyas which existed between 800 and 1470 AD. The fortress has high stone walls, narrow and walled alleys, circular stone houses adorned with rhomboid and zigzag ornaments. And yet the fortress was conquered by the Incas.

***Gocta Waterfall in Bongará*** - This is one of the highest waterfalls in Peru about 771 meters high. The height of the waterfall is not the only impressive thing about the Gocta. The "gallitos de las rocas", flora and fauna along with the monkeys are also sights to behold.

***Tucume*** - This is a vast desert site famous for its mysterious pyramids.

***Cordillera Blanca*** - Trek the mountains and gaze at the breathtaking mountain scenery.

***Piura*** - There is not much to see in this city but it offers Peru's finest cuisines. Although Lima is no known for the ceviche, locals argue that the dish was born in this city. If you find yourself here, you might as well give the conchas negras or black conch ceviche a try. It is absolute perfection.

***Cajamarca*** - It is spot less traveled by tourists but the locals are fond of Cajamarca because of its natural hot springs. Nestles in this small town are pre-Inca necropolis and pre-Columbian aqueduct ruins a well. Day tours only costs around $5 to $8. The town's cheese and chocolates are also among the hidden treasures of Peru.

***Mancora*** - If you're fond of pristine beaches, Mancora is a must-see. The beautiful waves attract surfers all over the world. You can relax on the white sand beaches and party at night.

***Lagoon of the Condors in Chachapoyas*** - Found in the Leymebamba district, this lagoon is also called Mummies Lagoon or Laguna de las Momias. That's because a tomb was discovered here. The tomb contained more than 200 well-preserced mummies. It is a wonder because the region has a rather damp and warm climate. Also found in the tomb are around 3,000 objects that belonged to the Chachapoya and Ica civilizations, pre-Inca time. Aside from being a site of discovery, the lagoon offers quite a view. To fully maximize the experience, hiring a guide is highly recommended.

# Chapter 8 – Where to Stay

From luxury to mid-range and budget hotels, accommodation in Peru varies. You can find the most convenient locations to the most unique features, extraordinary locations and best experiences regardless of your budget. Here are the hotels at the top of our list based on customer reviews, superb locations and fascinating features.

**Top End Hotels In Peru**

*JW Marriott Hotel Lima* - Located in the Miraflores district, this 5-star hotel boasts of a seafront location where guests can enjoy a spectacular view of the Pacific Ocean. At $155 a night, you get access to world class amenities including sauna and pool, bar and casino, executive lounge and an open-air tennis court. It is also located near the LarcoMar shopping mall.

Address: Malecon de La Reserva, 615 LimaPhone: +51-1-217-7000

Website: http://www.marriott.com/default.mi

*JW Marriott El Convento Cusco* - Situated at the heart of Cusco, this luxury hotel has a colonial atmosphere from the exterior to the front desk, the lobby, the themed rooms and outdoor courtyards. Room rates start at $259 a night.

Address: Esquina de la Calle Ruinas 432 y San Agustin, Cusco Peru

Phone: +51-84-582200

Website: http://www.marriott.com/hotels/travel/cuzmc-jw-marriott-el-convento-cusco/

***Casa Andina Arequipa, Arequipa*** - What do you think about staying at an 18th-century colonial mansion? The Casa Andina Arequipa provides more than a luxurious accommodation and excellent customer service. It is also declared as a National Historic Monument. Its spectacular courtyard is dream-like. Room rates at this hotel starts at $262 a night.

Address: Calle Ugarte 403, Arequipa, PE.

Phone: 51 (54) 226-907

Website: http://casa-andina.com/hoteles/hotel-arequipa-peru_casa-andina-private-collection/?lang=en

***Casa Andina Hotel Isla Suasi, Lake Titicaca*** - This hotel is truly one of a kind operating on solar energy, fully committed to cultural preservation and sustainable tourism. The entire structure was built using rocks, mud and wood. With its breathtaking views of the highest altitude along the lake, this hotel brings you closer to nature. It has wonderful terraced gardens and guests have access to various kinds of birds, around 7 vicuñas and 8 alpacas. You can ride a canoe, enjoy a relaxing massage and taste the best dishes at the hotel restaurant. The hotel rate starts at $349 which includes meals, beverages and boat transport to and from the island.

Address: Lago Titicaca, Moho Isla Suasi Puno Peru

Phone: +511 2139718

***Inkaterra Reserva Amazónica, Puerto Maldonado*** - This is another eco-friendly hotel situated in a rainforest reserve. It does not only provide you with comfortable accommodation and excellent service. It offers a unique experience. Inkaterra Reserva Amazónica has an in-house restaurant, spa and organic farm. Rates start at $612 for 2 days inclusive of all amenities.

Address: Rio Madre De Dios Km15, Puerto Maldonado, Peru

Phone: +51 1 6100400

Website: http://www.inkaterra.com/inkaterra/reserva-amazonica/

***Inkaterra Machu Picchu*** - Used to be known as the Machu Picchu Hotel, Inkaterra Machu Picchu is managed by the same people who established Inkaterra Reserva Amazónica. Inkaterra Machu Picchu embraces the beautiful historic sanctuary. It carefully blends this extraordinary natural setting with indigenous architecture. Within the property, you will find an organic farm adorned with a variety of orchids, begonias, ferns, native palms and wild strawberries.

The atmosphere is warm and friendly. You will be fascinated with the structure itself that is made from handmade bricks, stones, eucalyptus wood and mud bricks. Rates start at $517 a night.

Address: Aguas Calientes, Peru

Phone: +51 84 211122

Website: http://www.inkaterra.com/inkaterra/inkaterra-machu-picchu-pueblo-hotel/

***DCO Suites, Lounge & Spa*** - If you're stopping by Mancora, you better stay at DCO Suites Lounge & Spa. It's a little more expensive than other hotels around the area but if you want an experience of a lifetime, this is where you can have it. The hotel amenities include hot tub, massage and sauna with a restaurant that serves international dishes. The hotel is conveniently located only a few minutes away from the city center. It is also near the Piura and Tumbes airports. Rooms are available with beautiful sea views. Room rates start from $160.

Address: Ex Panamericana Norte Km 1214 + 800 Máncora Peru

Phone: +51 1 7071221

Website: http://www.hoteldco.com/english/index.html

## Best Mid-Range Hotels in Peru

The rates of mid-range hotels (2- and 3-star) in Peru are between $90 and $145. At this price range, you can still have the most pleasant accommodation and superb service. You just need to find the right place to stay. To help you out, here's a list.

***The Garden House Hotel Cusco*** - You won't find a lot of buzz about this Cusco hotel but it is truly a hidden treasure. The owners turned their family home into a cozy hotel. If you want a homey feel, this hotel provides such comfort. The hotel's exquisite garden has more than 1.500 rose bushes and native trees. It adds to the calming ambience. The best part is you get served with home cooked breakfast. Rates start at $145.

Address: Los Alamos B-6, Larapa, San Jeronimo, Cusco

Phone: (+51) 84 271 117

Website: http://www.cuscohouse.com/home.html

***Tierra Viva Miraflores Larco Hotel*** - Located along Bolivar Street near the Miraflores boardwalk, this 3-start hotel boasts of comfort, modern functionality and personalized service. The spacious terrace grants guest a view of the historic city center and the bohemian neighborhood. Room rates start from $90.

Address: Calle Bolivar 176-180, Miraflores. Lima, Peru

Phone: (+51) 01-6371003

Website: http://tierravivahoteles.com/tierra-viva-miraflores-larco/

***Tambo del Arriero Hotel Cusco*** - This 3-star hotel is located in an old colonial house. The love for history and culture is visible in every corner of the property. While everything feels colonial from the layout of the rooms, the murals, the patio and the courtyards with alcoves made of red brick and stone, the amenities are quite modern. The atmosphere is relaxing. It will be a pleasure to stay in this Cusco's little gem. Rates start from $90.

Address: 484 Nueva Alta Street, Cusco

Phone: (+51) 84 260 709

Website: http://www.tambodelarriero.com/

***Casa Andina Colca Lodge in Chivay*** - Located in Southern Peru, the lodge is perched at 12,000 feet. Close to the world famous Colca Valley, this Casa Andina Colca Lodge prides itself not only for having a great location but also for having a tranquil atmosphere. The stone casitas with their ceramic floors and thatched roofs leading to the beautiful garden patio is truly a sight to behold.

Casa Andina Colca Lodge also has a planetarium and clear atmosphere which is ideal for stargazing. In a nearby local village, you can learn to do traditional embroidery or treat yourself to an authentic piece of clothing straight from an artisan. In fact, you don't need to go far to grab a souvenir. The hotel has a local artisan who weaves in the fireplace lounge. You can get your souvenirs from here. Rates at the charming Casa Andina Colca Lodge start from $78.

Address: Chivay, Peru

Phone: +51 1 2139700

Website: http://casa-andina.com/

## High Budget Hotels in Peru

Even if you're on a tight budget, finding a safe, secure and comfortable accommodation in Peru should not be a problem. Options include 2- to 3-star hotels, hostels and B&Bs.

***Hotel San Antonio Abad*** - This charming 3-star hotel is conveniently located near to the city bus transit station. Despite its location, the ambience inside the hotel is surprisingly calm and quiet because of the soundproofed windows. The rooms in this bright-yellow mansion are clean and spacious. The staff is friendly. For an affordable hotel, it will exceed your expectations. Room rates start from $55 per night.

Address: Ramon Ribeyro, 301 Miraflores, Lima 18, Peru

Phone: +51 1 7097866

***Ecopackers Cusco*** - At only $12 a night per bed, this hostel in Cusco provides a safe and secure accommodation for backpackers. Situated near Plaza Regocijo, Ecopackers may be cheap but its rooms are clean, the beds are comfortable and the service is friendly. It has a sunbathing area, comfortable wicker lounges, a lovely courtyard, a bar and pool room.

Address: Calle Santa Teresa, 375 Cusco

Phone: +51 84 231800

Website: http://www.ecopackersperu.com/

***Ecopackers Machu Picchu*** – At $15.50 a night per bed, you get the same comforts that the Ecopackers in Cusco offers.

Address: Avenida Imperio de los Incas 136, Aguas Calientes Peru

Phone: ++51 1 5748000

Website: http://www.ecopackersperu.com/

***Gringo Bill's Hotel*** - In addition to the smart rooms, comfortable bedding, spacious bathrooms and modern amenities, Gringo Bill's Hotel boasts of being one of the original lodgings in Aguas Calientes. There are spa baths and private balconies in some rooms. All guests get access to the Pisco bar, the organic restaurant and a hot tub. Gringo Bill's Hotel lies close to the Manco Capac Main Square. Room rates start from $67 per night.

Address: Calle colla Raymi 104 Aguas Calientes Peru

Phone: +51 84 211046

Website: http://www.gringobills.com/site/eng/index.php

# Chapter 9 – Where to Eat

Peru is not only known for its ancient history and magnificent archeological complexes. The Peruvians also have the most diverse and finest cuisines in all of Latin America if not the whole world. When you taste exquisite Peruvian cuisine, it will be one of the highlights of your Peru trip.

**Chez Wong**

This restaurant in Lima is full of surprises. Chef Javier Wong does not offer a menu but customers can choose from either sweet or sour and hot or cold. Chef Wong cooked from his soul and the end product is simply delightful. The restaurant has varied clientele from a construction worker to Peruvian politicians. The cost of an average meal is around $45.

Address: Calle Enrique Leon Garcia 114 Lima Peru

Phone: +511 470 6217

Facebook Page: facebook.com/ChezJavierWong

**La Nueva Palomino, Arequipa**

This lovely family-run restaurant was established in the 1890s. Delicious dishes are prepared in the traditional way. The cooks use log fires. They use pestle and mortar to blend foods, not electric blenders. Among their best sellers include the prawn chowder with quinoa (chupe de camarones) and the chili peppers with pecans and minced beef filling (rocoto relleno). Average meal at this restaurant costs around $30.

Address: Leoncio Prado 122 Arequipa Peru

Phone: +51 54252393

Facebook Page: facebook.com/LaNuevaPalomino/

## El Mercado, Lima

This Lima restaurant is best known for their ceviche. Keeping up with the tradition, El Mercado is only open at lunchtime and is always jampacked. Headed by Chef Rafael Osterling, the restaurant is highly regarded for their flavourful food and high standard service. They will give you a fine dining experience at a much more reasonable price. In addition to the ceviche, El Mercado's fish roe sandwich and grilled octopus are also to die for. Average meal costs around $60.

Address: Hipólito Unanue 203 Lima Peru

Phone: +511 221 1322

Website: rafaelosterling.pe

## San Pedro Market, Cusco

This indoor market has a lot to offer to a hungry passerby. There are excellent food stalls inside that sell a variety of foods from breads to fruit juices. Don't miss them out on your way to Machu Picchu.

## Al Frio y Al Fuego, Iquitos

It's a restaurant that floats on the Itaya river. They have the best ceviche made of paiche fish. Many travelers rave about this restaurant whose specialty is river seafood. Average meal at Al Frio y Al Fuego is around $38.

Address: Avenida La Marina N 134-B Iquitos Peru

Phone: +51 65 607474

Website: alfrioyalfuego.com

## La Tia Grimanesa, Lima

The owner, Grimanesa Vargas, rose to fame because of her legendary anticuchos or beef-heart skewers. Marinated in garlic, red wine vinegar and smokey chili, the anticuchos in La Tia Grimanesa is the best in Lima and probably in all of Peru.

For such a popular restaurant, La Tia Grimanesa is quite affordable. An average meal costs around $15.

Address: Jr Ignacio Merino 466 Lima Peru

Phone: +51 99 849 3137

Website: grimanesavargasanticuchos.com

**Huacatay**

If you want to have a genuine Peruvian culinary experience, you need to hunt down this restaurant found in a little house in a narrow street. Their tender alpaca steak with quinoa risotto, port reduction sauce and spiral potato chips toppings is sublime. If you want to have a simple yet lovely dinner, Huacatay serves it just right with the warm ambience and friendly service. The average meal price is at $53.

Address: Arica 620 Urubamba , Peru

Phone: +51 84 20 1790

Website: http://www.elhuacatay.com/

**Cicciolina**

Dubbed as Cusco's best restaurant, this fine restaurant housed in a colonial courtyard mansion, serves international cuisine. The food is just as sophisticated as the environment. Their best dishes include the tender lamb, squid-ink pasta, charred octopus, marinated olives and crispy polenta squares served with cured rabbit. It comes highly recommended. An average meal at Cicciolina costs around $65.

Address: Triunfo 393 2nd fl Cuzco Peru

Phone: +51 84 23 9510

Website: https://www.cicciolinacuzco.com/

# Chapter 10 – Where to Shop

Visiting Peruvian markets is another interesting experience. It is a reflection of local culture. And you cannot leave without taking souvenirs. You will find intricate weavings, beautiful textiles, embroidered items, carved wood and other craft goods in these local markets.

**Mercado Indio**

You will find all sorts of interesting stuff here from Cuzco school knock-off canvases to alpaca rugs and clay pottery pre-Columbian style. Shop around and you will find plenty to love to take home.

Address: Av Petit Thouars 5245 Miraflores Lima Peru

**Mercado San Pedro**

This indoor market does not only house a variety of food stalls. There is a wide range of products from clothes to incense and spells. You will be overwhelmed with all the vibrant colors, sizes and shapes this market has to offer.

Address: Plazoleta San Pedro Cuzco Peru

**Feria Dominical**

If you are looking for something more unique like arts and crafts, you will find plenty in this Sunday craft market. Here you will find the beautiful weavings, textiles, wood carvings, ceramics and embroidered items. The products are brought here from various villages. If you don't have the time to visit the Río Mantaro valley, you can still get a souvenir of their famous mates burilados or carved gourds at Feria Dominical.

Address: Huancavelica Huancayo, Peru

**Mercado de Artesania**

It's probably the most popular among tourists and it is the biggest one in the region too. Needless to say, the items sold in the market vary from food to fresh produce to local handmade products and craft goods. The market is open for business daily but if you want to avoid big crowds, you should schedule your shopping on Monday, Wednesday, Friday or Saturday.

Address: Pisac Peru

**Mercado de Chinchero**

Less crowded but just as exquisite, Mercado de Chinchero is open for business on Tuesday, Thursday and Sunday. The most interesting thing here is locals still practice bartering or trueco. It is a rare opportunity you certainly should not miss. There are various produce and other interesting items you will find in this charming market.

Address: Chinchero Peru

**Mercado Modelo**

This market is famous for all sorts of reasons. However, it is visited by a huge number of tourists and locals for the mercado de brujos or witch doctor's market located in the southwest area. You will find the most interesting items and concoctions here from huge piles of aromatic herbs to hallucinogenic cacti, from vials of tonics to snake skins, from amulets to whale bones.

Address: Arica btwn Balta & Cugilevan Chiclayo Peru

# Chapter 11 – When to Celebrate

With such a deep history, wealthy in natural reserves, delicious food, the best in the world and vibrant culture, the Peruvians have lots of reasons to celebrate. And they do. Festivals in this country are guided by their commitment to religion and spiritual heritage. You can experience Peruvian culture first hand in full living color. Join in the fun at Peruvian festivals like no other. Here's the top list of Peru's best festivals and biggest events of the year.

## Inti Raymi in Cusco

Also known as the 'Festival of the Sun,' Inti Raymi is a yearly celebration held on the 24th of June. It is considered the most important event in Cusco. Locals and tourists alike gather in the city to party in the streets. The celebration kicks off with a re-enactment of the Inca's Sacsaywamán winter-solstice festival. Although it is now heavily commercialized, the colorful costumes of street dancers, the elaborate parade and the pageantry held at Sacsaywamán are still a joy to watch.

The Inca spearheads the celebration

## Q'oyoriti in Cusco

Although overshadowed by the Inti Raymi festival, the Q'oyoriti is a spectacular event in its own right. Every year on a Tuesday before Corpus Christi, the Peruvians gather at the foot of the Ausangate to re-live traditional Andean rites. It usually falls in late May or early June in Cusco.

Local indigenous groups gather in honor of ancient Andean traditions

## El Señor de los Milagros in Lima

A religious event honoring Christ from the Nazarenas church, locals hold a massive religious parade along Centro Historico. It happens every 18th of October. In preparation for the procession, the entire city of Lima is draped in purple. There are other processions held on Sundays of October as well although much smaller in scale.

> Christ of the Nazarene is taken to a procession by purple cloaked devotees

## La Virgen de la Candelaria in Puno

Following the religious calendar, this festival is focused on the week of Candlemas. The spectacular event is spread out around the actual date of the Candlemas. It usually occurs between the 2nd and 18th of February. If the Candlemas week is between Sunday and Tuesday, celebration starts on the previous Saturday. On the other hand, if it is between Wednesday and Friday, celebration keeps going until the following Saturday.

## Semana Santa in Ayacucho

Being a religious country, the Peruvians do not just focus on Easter Sunday. They follow the religious tradition of the Holy Week in the Roman Catholic calendar. It is considered to be the finest religious festival in the country and people from all over the world join in every year.

The event kicks off on the Friday before Palm Sunday. On this day, a parade is held in honor of the Our Lady of Sorrows (La Virgen de los Dolores). As is customary, pebbles are fired on bystanders to commemorate the inflicting of "sorrows." The event goes on for 10 days until Easter. Religious rites, processions and religious services continue in the succeeding days.

The Peruvians greet Easter with a bang. Saturday before Easter, they pull an all-night party that goes on until dawn. There are fireworks, loud music, concerts, sporting and street events. In addition to the religious traditions, there are folk-dancing competitions, art shows, preparation of traditional meals and agricultural fairs during the Semana Santa. That means, there is plenty to experience during this time of the year in Peru.

## Carnaval in Cajamarca

This has nothing to do with religion but the Carnaval festivities are probably the most popular and wildest events in Peru. If you want to experience rowdy Peruvian party, you should drop by Cajamarca before the Lenten season.

# Conclusion

Once again thank you for choosing *Lost Travelers*!

I hope this book was able to provide you with the best travel tips when visiting Peru.

*And we hope you enjoy your travels.*

"Travel Brings Power And Love Back To Your Life"

- Rumi

Finally, if you enjoyed this book, then I'd like to ask you for a favor, would you be kind enough to leave a review for this book on Amazon? It'd be greatly appreciated!

- Simply search the keywords "Peru Lost Travelers" on Amazon or go to our Author page "Lost Travelers" to review.

Your satisfaction is important to us! If you were not happy with the book please email us with the title, your comment and suggestion so we may consider any improvements and serve you better in the next edition.

- Email: SevenTreeImprove@gmail.com

Thank you and good luck!

# NOTES

# NOTES

# NOTES

# NOTES

# Preview Of 'Vietnam: The Ultimate Vietnam Travel Guide By A Traveler For A Traveler

Modern-day Vietnamese trace their ancestry to the Lac people who founded a Bronze Age civilization in the first millennium BC near the fertile Red River Delta in the north. In the third century BC, a Chinese military adventurer conquered the Vietnamese kingdom of Van Lang and incorporated the Red River Delta into his expanding realm in Southern China. China eventually integrated Vietnam into its Chinese empire a hundred years later.

The more than 1,000 years of Chinese rule wrought significant changes in Vietnam's culture and society as its people were introduced to Chinese art, literature, architecture, language, ideas, religion, political system and social institutions. Ethnic Vietnamese were torn between their attraction to Chinese culture and their desire to resist the colonist's political grip. In AD 939, however, Vietnamese rebels took advantage of China's political chaos and restored national independence.

The Vietnamese Empire known as Dai Viet flourished, expanded steadily southward, and gradually formed its own institutions over a period of several hundred years. China periodically made attempts to regain control of Vietnam, but they were repulsed under the dynasty of the Ly (1000-1225AD) and the Tran (1225-1400AD). The expansion to the south continued at the expense of Champa, their southern neighbor and a civilization which flourished in South Vietnam during China's domination of the north. The Indian-influenced Champa kingdom was founded and ruled by non-Vietnamese people, the Chams.

Chinese rule was restored in the early 15$^{th}$ century, but a national revolt led by the Le Loi cut the reign short. This led to the formation of the Le Dynasty, which lasted from 1428 to 1788. By the 17$^{th}$ century, the Le Dynasty gained complete control of Southern Vietnam and ruled over the entire Mekong River Delta. The Le leadership, however, would later slip into a civil strife between two warring royal families, the Trinh in northern Vietnam and the Nguyen in the south. The political turmoil happened at a time when European explorers were just starting to extend their missionary and commercial activities in the East, including Southeast Asia.

A peasant uprising led by the Tay Son brothers overthrew the Nguyen and the Trinh in 1771 and united the country under the leadership of the most competent among the Tay Son brothers, Emperor Nguyen Hue. His reign was short, however, as his kingdom was subdued by a military force organized by a Nguyen prince with the help of a French missionary bishop. The victory ushered in the Nguyen Dynasty (1802-1945) and reunified the country under the leadership of Emperor Gia Long. The alliance between France and the Nguyen dynasty, however, soon turned sour as both Gia Long and his son and successor, Minh Mang, refused to grant missionary and commercial privileges to France. TO BE CONTINUED!

Check out the rest of Vietnam: The Ultimate Vietnam Travel Guide on Amazon by simply searching it.

# Check Out Our Other Books

Below you'll find some of our other popular books that are on Amazon and Kindle as well. Simply search the titles below to check them out. Alternatively, you can visit our author page (Lost Travelers) on Amazon to see other work done by us.

- Vienna: The Ultimate Vienna Travel Guide By A Traveler For A Traveler
- Barcelona: The Ultimate Barcelona Travel Guide By A Traveler For A Traveler
- London: The Ultimate London Travel Guide By A Traveler For A Traveler
- Istanbul: The Ultimate Istanbul Travel Guide By A Traveler For A Traveler
- Vietnam: The Ultimate Vietnam Travel Guide By A Traveler For A Traveler
- Peru: The Ultimate Peru Travel Guide By A Traveler For A Traveler
- Australia: The Ultimate Australia Guide By A Traveler For A Traveler
- Japan: The Ultimate Japan Travel Guide By A Traveler For A Traveler
- New Zealand: The Ultimate New Zealand Travel Guide By A Traveler For A Traveler

- Dublin: The Ultimate Dublin Travel Guide By A Traveler For A Traveler

- Thailand: The Ultimate Thailand Travel Guide By A Traveler For A Traveler

- Iceland: The Ultimate Iceland Travel Guide By A Traveler For A Traveler

- Santorini: The Ultimate Santorini Travel Guide By A Traveler For A Traveler

- Italy: The Ultimate Italy Travel Guide By A Traveler For A Traveler

You can simply search for these titles on the Amazon website to find them.

Made in United States
North Haven, CT
09 December 2023